High Fashion in Stuart Times

Andrew Brownfoot

Tarquin Publications

James 1	1603-1625
Charles 1	1625-1649
Commonwealth	1649-1653
Oliver Cromwell	1653-1658
Richard Cromwell	1658-1659
Charles II	1660-1685
James II	1685-1688
William & Mary	1689-1702
Anne	1702-1714

The Stuart era in England lasted for just over one hundred years. It was a time when violence, immoderate extravagance and the most astonishing changes in fashion combined with fierce religious and political intolerance. Continental Europe was torn by war and every year for the thirty years from 1618 to 1648, the approach of spring was a signal for yet another season of bloodshed to start.

England, by contrast, was seemingly immune from this plague of war. Under James I and the opening years of the reign of Charles I from 1625 to 1637, the realm was a haven of peace and prosperity. King Charles I and Queen Henrietta Maria surrounded themselves with people of culture and refinement, connoisseurs of art, literature and music who dressed in a high-waisted romantic elegance that has never been surpassed.

During these years whenever English courtiers were seen by foreigners, they caused astonishment by the luxury of their dress and their lavish styles. Charles's favourite, the Duke of Buckingham, set the trend when he and Charles first paid a visit to the French court. Dressed in a suit entirely covered with pearls of great value, Buckingham illustrated his wealth by having the pearls sewn on in such a way that they dropped off as he walked. The Duke passed through the astonished French courtiers apparently careless of their loss. They, however, were not ashamed, even in the presence of their Queen, to retrieve them.

Although Charles set a new standard of personal morality at court, his behaviour in governing the kingdom was often devious and arrogant. He tried to impose his will upon all and the disputes between the King and Parliament grew ever more serious. Emotions ran higher and higher. They were fired by fierce disagreements over money and religion and finally, in 1642, the disputes spilled over into civil war. The fighting ended with a victory for Parliament and the beheading of the King in 1649.

A Commonwealth was declared and at first it appeared to offer more equality and a sharing of wealth. However, it did not work out well. Parliament split into factions, each member determined to undermine his rivals and all refusing to step down and allow a new parliament to be elected. They squabbled and quibbled over the smallest proposal and nothing was achieved. Finally in a fit of frustration and anger, Cromwell stormed into the House of Commons with a troop of soldiers and forcibly ejected the members.

He then ruled for five years as Lord Protector. This was dictatorship and the over-zealous activities of the puritans and the army became incredibly unpopular. Cromwell died in 1658 and his son Richard was then made Lord Protector. After only four months he was unable to continue. Eventually it was decided to turn the clock back and to invite Charles Stuart to become King Charles II. This *Restoration* of the royal family ushered in a new era of fashion and high society.

These four pictures give a general impression of how fashionable silhouettes changed during Stuart Times.

Around 1634

Around 1645

High Fashion and Society

Contrary to popular belief, fashions continued to change with no lack of extravagance or invention throughout the civil wars in both Europe and England. Here, most wealthy parliamentary supporters were as flamboyant as their royalist opponents, dressing in all the latest styles and colours. For the most part the only way you could tell which side anyone was fighting for was by the colour of his silken sash. We have come to use the names of *Cavalier* and *Roundhead* as the simplest way of describing the royalists and the parliamentarians. However, originally these labels were terms of abuse. Roundhead at first referred only to a group of London apprentice recruits. They cut off their long hair as a mark of their regiment and were thought to look ridiculous. Cromwell always wore his hair at the fashionable length, just breaking on the shoulders

For most people, changes to everyday life following the execution of Charles I and during the Commonwealth, were not great. Theatres and other places of entertainment were closed to placate the puritan elements in the country but private entertainments continued to be popular. Oliver Cromwell, who was king in all but name, was a tolerant man and particularly fond of music. He was not the grim dictator of some popular histories.

The royalist cavaliers, for the most part, escaped to the Continent and lived as best they could with the meagre incomes they managed to obtain after the victorious Parliament sequestrated their property. Houses, estates and furnishings were taken and redistributed, leaving many families at home with no means of support. It was the women who were left to struggle in the courts to clear their husband's name and retrieve such of their property as they could.

By 1660, the majority of people were thoroughly tired of Bible thumping on Sundays, no maypole dancing or public entertainments and they were delighted to find King Charles II restored to power. Costume blossomed into a full blown fantasy of lace, ribbon and ostrich feathers that completely disguised the corpulent figure of an over-indulgent man and revealed the treasures of cosseted and ambitious women.

Life was fun once more. It was corrupt. But that was no different from what happened during the period of puritan rule. What was different was the return to dancing, theatres and open public enjoyment. For the first time women could act on the stage and some were even accepted as professional playwrights.

New times required new plays. Plays that reflected the preoccupations of a hedonistic liberated aristocracy with money now burning holes in their pockets and also included those eager to take part in the high life offered at Court. Spectacular scenic effects were imported from France and staged in the new indoor theatres. These were crammed with mechanical devices and were used for grand retellings of classical stories of gods and kings, queens and tragic heroic love. Even better, and certainly we think so today, were the comedies of manners in which people could watch and laugh at their own society.

It was not until the 1680s, however, that the *Restoration Comedies*, as we now call them, truly developed from the French models of Molière. Playwrights like William Congreve and Sir John Vanbrugh mirrored in their plays the elegant, mannered amorality of the Court and produced plays which are still greatly appreciated today.

Sadly, the political honeymoon and truce did not last. When King James II who was Catholic, inherited the throne in 1685, the old religious intolerances erupted again. Even his own daughters, Mary and Anne, conspired against him. James was deserted by almost everyone and left the country in disguise leaving the Throne vacant for Mary and her Dutch husband William of Orange. They were crowned as joint rulers after what became known later as *The Glorious Revolution,* much to the delight of the English Protestants.

The serious new King and his tall vivacious wife brought with them many new fashions in furnishing and gardening, and did nothing to halt the riotous extravagance of the previous reigns. In fact a display of wealth at Court was considered politically essential to maintain the respect of rival nations. To be accepted and successful in Society, you had to be considered part of what was then fashionably called *The Quality*.

Anyone outside this privileged group was considered worthy only of contempt and had no opportunity for social advancement. Acquisition of fine clothes and the elaborate manners of the French Court would, however, give entry to a royal palace or to any fashionable grandee's house, with all the opportunities that this presented.

High Fashion in Stuart Times was indeed a passport to wealth, power and influence.

Around 1666

Around 1690

Armour

Armour was still useful in the gruesome hand to hand fighting that formed the major part of any battle at this time. Firearms were difficult and unreliable and had a very short range. However, throughout the Stuart period their efficiency improved and full armour soon became an encumbrance rather than a protection. At the beginning of the Civil War, the King and others did wear it but probably only to show their rank. Many portraits of the period do show generals and admirals in armour but on the battlefield after 1642, the most practical combination was a cuirass over a buff coat. A helmet or *pot* was also useful. It provided some protection and did not restrict mobility too much. During the civil war the cuirass conformed to the high waisted styles of fashionable clothing and also to quality regulations; each piece was tested, or proved, with a single bullet fired from a stipulated distance. The dents are clearly visible even in the portraits of the period.

Baldric

A baldric could be either a sash or a belt worn hanging diagonally across the body, usually from the right shoulder to the left hip. Before uniforms had become standardised, a baldric (of silk for officers) was worn to indicate the allegiance or regiment of its wearer. Since breeches in the 1630's were often still attached to the high waisted doublet, it was necessary to wear a baldric made of leather, or some other strong material, to support the sword. This was considered better than spoiling the silhouette with a belt. Once the breeches had become separated from the doublet and were hung from the hips, then sword belts returned to favour. By the 1680's the baldric was forgotten by fashionable men and never reappeared.

Bands & Band Strings

Collars continued to be called bands, as they had been in Shakespeare's time. During the reign of Charles I, men wore many styles but the most typical fell from the neck and spread out over the shoulders. A band was always worn over the top of any coat or cloak and frequently displayed the most beautiful lace edge. These collars were tied at the front with strings called band strings which often had elaborate and expensive tassel ends. During this period, women also wore a variety of beautiful arrangements and combinations of collars.

Banquet - see **Dessert**

Beards & Moustaches

Beards were fashionable in the first half of the century, particularly the style said to have been created by King Louis XIII of France. The King became an enthusiastic amateur barber and decided to shave all but the tuft growing under the lower lip of several courtiers. Later beards were no longer worn by men of fashion but a narrow moustache continued to be popular. By the 1680's even that disappeared and for more than a hundred years, fashionable men were clean shaven.

Bodice

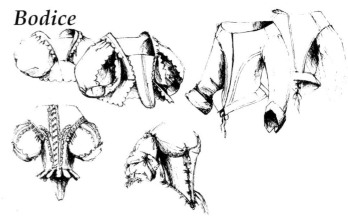

The name bodice originates from the Elizabethan *Pair of Bodies* which was an early form of corset worn under the gown. By the 1620's, the fashionable high-waisted look required less boning and so the bodice could be worn as a top garment. Although the waistline descended in the 1640's, the bodice established itself as the supremely elegant outer garment. It then regained and increased its boning to achieve the rigid elegance of court dress.

Boots

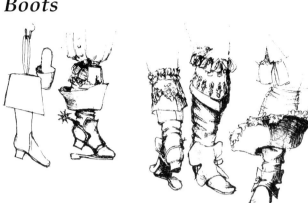

This violent age, so typified by the civil wars in Europe and in England, made military styles into high fashion. Boots and spurs were worn by almost every man on most occasions, even at Court. As with all fashion items, boots rapidly lost their practicality. To protect their elegant heels from the muddy ground, boots were worn inside special slippers called pantobles. The resulting difficulty in walking, coupled with an admired clacking sound made by the boot heel on the sole of the pantoble led to the development of a style that combined pantoble and boot into one. Many of these *slap-soled* boots have survived to the present day, whereas the original sets of separate pantobles and boots have been lost. Obviously the pantobles were the first to wear out and were then thrown away, leaving only the matching boots. Boots such as these were thigh-length but usually turned first down and then up into a double fold below the knee. As time went by, the tops became wider and wider until by the late 40's it became necessary to walk with an extraordinary rolling gait in order to put one leg in front of the other. This swagger became fashionable in itself and men continued to sway from side to side, even though they were not wearing boots that required it.

Busk

The name given to the long extra strong bone slipped into a pocket to keep the front of the bodice straight and unbending.

Buskins

Buskins were theatrical boots, especially popular in court masques and entertainments, usually in imitation of Greek or Roman sandals. They are frequently depicted in paintings and portraits of the period.

Cadenettes

From about 1620 to 1650, it was fashionable for men to wear their hair longer on the left side than the right. This *love-lock* was sometimes plaited and decorated with ribbon in the manner invented by Cadenet, the fashion-obsessed brother of the Duc de Luynes.

Capes & Cloaks

Capes were worn by all men of fashion on almost all occasions until about 1675. Circular in shape, they usually matched the doublet and were lined with an even more extravagant material. In the 1630's and 40's, the cape was commonly thrown over the left shoulder and the bottom edge pulled up to reveal the lining. If the doublet and breeches were not of matching fabric then the cape was often made with the lining matching the doublet and the outside matching the breeches. For extra warmth in winter, larger cloaks were worn by both sexes and could be luxuriously lined in fur.

Casaque & Cassock

The casaque was a military form of cloak made up of separate sections which could be turned into a sleeved coat by the clever arrangement of buttons. The French name sometimes became Anglicised to cassock and was a popular garment used for riding. Cassock is also the name generally given to the loose fitting over-garment worn by clerics and choristers. However, in the contemporary description of the masque at Bolsover Castle, the name was used, I believe, to describe garments that were intended to represent the soft drapery of the ancient Greek chiton.

Coats

Originally a military garment, the coat seems to have been introduced from Eastern Europe during the Thirty Years War. There were many variations of these loose fitting overcoats and in 1666, King Charles II announced that all gentlemen of the Court should wear a new form, black 'Persian Vests' trimmed with white. Strictly speaking vests were what we would now call sleeved waistcoats. When they were worn under the Persian Coat, the complete suit could then be referred to as a Persian Vest. In the end Charles decided that the courtiers looked too much like magpies, so black and white was no longer obligatory. These coats became more elegantly shaped and continued in fashion for well over a century.

Corsets or Stays

When the mantua was introduced, its loose style required a boned undergarment, a corset, to achieve the fashionable long-bodied look. Even when the mantua had gained the formality essential at Court, it was never boned itself but was *stayed* (pinned securely) to the armour-like corset underneath.

Cravats

The cravat developed from the military habit of tying the large lace collars with a ribbon at the throat, so keeping them from blowing across the face. They were named after Louis XIV's Croat mercenary soldiers. In the 1660's scarves of fine linen with lace ends began to replace collars. They were wrapped around the neck and then tied in various ways at the throat. Cravats superseded bands for all occasions after about 1670.

Cuirass - see Armour

Dessert or Banquet

Dessert has come to mean the fruit or sweetmeats that we eat at the end of a large meal. What we now call a banquet was always known as a *feast* in the Elizabethan and Stuart period. To them a banquet or a dessert meant the same thing. It was served when people left the main table at the end of the feast, so that it could be cleared and space made for dancing. They moved elsewhere where they were given sweetmeats and fruit. The word banquet comes from the French for a small table on which the dessert was often presented and dessert is from the French verb *desservir* which means to clear the table.

Drawers

Men's underpants, made to a simple pattern similar to Boxer Shorts nowadays. Because of their long skirts and petticoats, women rarely wore the female equivalent, knickers.

Doublet

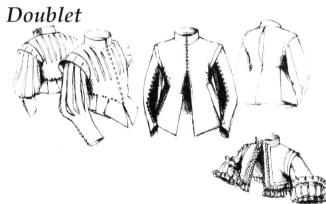

Doublets were originally introduced in the 14th century as a practical protection from chaffing caused by the cuirass. Like so many practical military items they soon became fashionable masculine attire. Consequently they changed with every whim of fashion. Doublets were always tight fitting and padded, at least on the belly and often lavishly decorated. By 1600 the doublet was worn by every male over the age of five. However, from the 1620's the fashionable doublet began to shrink, getting ever shorter in the waist. As it did so, trousers or breeches became high waisted and continued to be supported from the doublet. This style was very uncomfortable and when King Charles II returned to England in 1660, the doublet had been reduced to a ridiculously tiny separate garment which was worn, it seemed, only to support its elbow length sleeves. It then disappeared from fashion history, never to return.

Fontanges

A form of head-dress introduced by Mlle de Fontanges, the beautiful but short-lived mistress of Louis XIV. These lace bonnets consisted of a high tower of lace at the front and trailing lappets framing the face. By the 1680's the height had increased so much that to be fashionable, it needed the support of wiring. A profusion of ribbon was then added to the back of the towering display.

Galants & Gallants

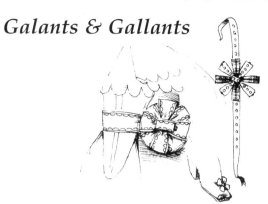

Galants were made-up rosettes of ribbon that were placed about the costume, particularly at the waist, arm or knee. They became extremely popular in the 1630's and 40's. Although galants came in all colours, red was especially popular.

Gallants, on the other hand, were fashionable young men who were attentive to women.

Hair Styles

Throughout the Stuart period it was fashionable for men to have long hair. Since this was difficult to manage, the majority resorted to wearing wigs. Women also sometimes wore wigs, but this was much less common. Women were comparatively conservative in dressing their hair although the many portraits that have survived show a wide variety of different styles. Early in the Stuart period they distributed their hair into four sections. On the forehead there was a small fringe, on the sides an effect like spaniel's ears was created with hair that was either frizzled or curled into shape. Finally, the rest of the hair was pulled back and arranged into a bun at the back of the head. Towards the end of the period the hair at the sides was curled and linked with the fringe to create high towering arrangements. As fashions changed, the bun at the back changed shape from round to a wide Staffordshire knot and back again. However severe the bun might seem, it was always possible to allow one or two locks of hair to escape and curl seductively over the shoulders.

Lappet

In fashion terms it was a strip of folded cloth or lace which often was attached to head-dresses. It also means a fold of skin or flesh!

Lawn

A fine high quality linen, used mainly for shirts and chemises.

Mantua

This style first appeared about 1670 as a loose informal gown for relaxing with close friends. It provided an acceptable relief from the rigours of tight boning. However, like so many other popular fashions, the mantua rapidly developed into a formal garment. The loose folds held at the waist with a ribbon soon became formalised into pleats at each side of a stomacher. By the 1690's the mantua was standard wear at Court on all but the most formal occasions.

Patches

Patches or false beauty spots were fashionable from the 1660's onwards. They were made of black velvet or taffeta and cut into a variety of shapes, usually ready-pasted for easy fixing to the skin. What probably started out as a way of hiding smallpox scars became an obsession. Both sexes were addicted to their use and the placing of the patches became a secret language. The French called them *mouches* or flies.

Perukes or Wigs

During the second half of the 17th century, elaborate wigs or perukes (from the French *perruques*) were particularly fashionable for men. Women tended to prefer hair-pieces which they then added to their natural hair. In the 1660's men's wigs were massive. At first they were wide and rather flat across the top of the head but as women's head-dresses became higher so did men's wigs. They also became longer and were very expensive items indeed to maintain. The necessity to *cover* or wear a hat in formal situations, often caused damage to them. To avoid unexpected bills for wig repairs, it was customary to pay a quarterly fee, a *quarterage*, to a barber or wig maker. So high in status and prestigious did the wearing of a large wig become that even today important people are still known as *bigwigs*.

Persian Vest - see Coats

Petticoats

Skirts which had no front opening were called petticoats and the number worn differed according to the time of year, with flannel petticoats being especially popular in winter. In Stuart times, our word *skirt* simply meant the edging at the bottom of a petticoat. Until the 1670's, petticoats were generally decorated with lines of braid or lace placed just above the hem and arranged vertically at the front. During the eighties and nineties, horizontal arrangements of braid, tassels and fringes became the most fashionable form of decoration.

Pot

This was the popular name for a helmet during the civil wars. The *lobster tailed pot* or *trooper's pot* had developed in Europe during the Thirty Years War and since it offered a certain degree of effective protection, it was adopted elsewhere. Contrary to popular belief, it was worn by the cavalry of both sides in the English civil wars.

Quarterage - see **Perukes**

Ribbons & Ribbon Knots

People of the 17th century had an extraordinary passion for ribbon. This was most evident in the 1660's when clusters of ribbons were attached to every available surface and object.

Rhinegreaves or Petticoat Breeches

Men's breeches had developed from the open bottomed galligaskins of Shakespeare's time, and by the 1640's the leg openings had become wider. By the 1660's they had become so wide that they were more like two short skirts. Not only was it possible to make the mistake of putting both legs through one opening, but also to be totally unaware of it!

The Order of Saint-Esprit

This was the most coveted order of Knighthood in France. It was formed in 1578 to rival the English *Order of the Garter*.

Shirts

Made of fine linen, shirts were simply constructed but lavishly trimmed with lace. From the 1630's, as the doublet declined in size, the shirt became more important and by the 1660's lavish displays of fine linen were essential for a man of fashion. Shirt sleeves were made extremely long and full so that they could be gathered and puffed at intervals down the arm.

Shoes

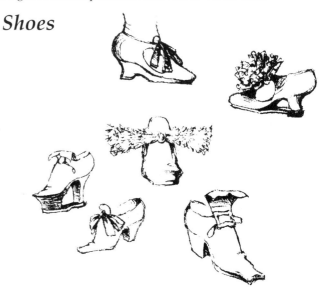

Early in the 17th century there was little difference between the sexes in the styles of shoe worn by fashionable people, although women's shoes tended to have more pointed toes. High heels became increasingly popular. During the 1640's, shoes usually had a rosette decoration to conceal the instep fastening. This style gave way, first to wired ribbon bows and then to small metal buckles, often jewelled. Fashionable shoes were made with *slap-soles*, just as boots were and for the same reason. It is curious that the exaggerated tongue of modern trainers had a close counterpart in the 17th century.

Stockings or Hose

Covering the lower leg and supported below the knee with garters, stockings were most fashionably made of knitted silk. During the reigns of both Charles I and Charles II, it was considered stylish to wear them wrinkled. This was thought to delineate the elegant form of the calf and ankle. When boots were fashionable, additional *boot hose* were worn to protect the fine silk stockings from damage by the friction of the boot. Boot hose themselves then became fashionable accessories and became trimmed with the inevitable lace! In fact, the way that they flopped around the leg was so much admired that boot hose were often worn with shoes alone, totally ignoring their original purpose.

The Daily Journals

&

Pull-up Scenes

1634 to 1694

*Let us now meet the four diarists and through their journals,
glimpse fashionable life in Court circles at this time in history.
The writers are imaginary and their journals are invented but
they comment on the events of the time and their concern
for fashion mirrors that of the real people they meet.*

Lucy Townsend

Ralph Townsend

Hortense Townsend

Henry Townsend

In 1634, Lucy Townsend is Lady in Waiting to the Countess of Newcastle. Lucy's husband is seldom in England spending long periods fighting in Germany for whoever will hire him during what became known as the *Thirty Years War*. With her young sons Ralph and Henry, she meets the King and Queen at a court masque at Bolsover Castle and her first diary entry is of this event.

In 1642, the Civil War begins and her son Ralph, although he is only 16, takes part in the battle of Edge Hill. He is lucky to escape with his life and does not enjoy the experience at all. After that he takes care to avoid being involved in any further fighting but does attend Court in Oxford, during the period when it is the headquarters of the King. When the Royalists lose the war and the King is executed, Ralph has to flee abroad. The family property is sequestrated by Parliament but his mother is in no danger of arrest. Women are not considered responsible for the actions of their menfolk.

While Ralph is in Paris, he meets his future wife Hortense and after the Restoration in 1660 when Charles II is welcomed back as King, they too are able to return and to live in London. They are fortunate that their house just escapes the *Great Fire of London* in 1666, but far from being grateful for this piece of good luck, they are dismayed by the destructive effect the soot and dust has on their clothes.

Of much more concern to Ralph than the Great Fire is the introduction of the Persian Vest, a dramatic fashion change which catches him completely unawares.

After the *Glorious Revolution*, which brings William and Mary to the Throne in 1689, things finally settle down and life again becomes peaceful and prosperous, at least in the higher echelons of society. Our final diarist, their son Henry, usually called Henpen, is an artist and he writes in 1694. Through his diary we hear of the unfortunate death of Queen Mary.

The Great Stuart Diarists

Our diarists were fictional, but two of the very greatest diarists were alive at this time. Through their writings and observations, we have a very good idea of what Stuart Society was like.

John Evelyn
(1620-1706)

Most famous for his Diary, John Evelyn was one of those fortunate people who went through life without ever having to earn his living. He was a younger son and so, when his father died in 1637, his brother inherited the estate. The seventeen year old John, having completed his studies at Oxford, travelled on the continent. When the civil war started, he returned to England and joined the royalist army. Although he did not lack courage, he soon realised that military life was not for him. He resumed his travels, visiting the Netherlands, France and Italy, learning the languages and enjoying the riches of art, music and architecture he found on the way. In 1647 he married Mary Browne, the daughter of the English ambassador in Paris.

He was on friendly terms with King Charles II because of their mutual interest in science and gardening. John Evelyn's cultivated knowledge of the arts and fashion, seems to have placed him in the unofficial role of Court adviser in these matters. It is he whom we have to thank for introducing Grinling Gibbons, the great sculptor and woodcarver, to his wealthy patrons at Court. He also published a paper appealing for measures to cut down the amount of smoke in London. He was a rare man indeed for his time. Seemingly uninterested in social advancement, he refused the offer of being made a Knight of the Bath. He also steadfastly refused to take up any paid official appointment.

Samuel Pepys
(1633-1703)

With a father who was a successful and well connected tailor, it is not surprising that Samuel Pepys was extremely interested in his clothes. No one could have guessed, however, that he would also prove to be one of the greatest administrators of his age. Even more surprising is the fact that his personal diary should prove to be one of the richest sources of information about the history of England in the second half of the 17th Century. He walked through the City of London, with bonfires at every corner, when Charles II was coming home. He was there, observing and writing his comments, on the ship that sailed to collect the King from Holland. Pepys knew most of the people involved in government and the Court and hated the lack of morals at every level of society.

His description of the Plague of 1665, and the Great Fire of London the following year are probably the most detailed and moving accounts we have of these horrific events. Samuel Pepys was the very ideal of what we would now call an efficient and industrious civil servant. His work in the Navy Board stamped out corruption and ensured proper payments and efficient delivery of ship building materials, and food supplies for all the King's ships. Pepys stopped writing his diary at the age of 36 because he thought he was going blind. In fact, he never lost his sight and, although he frequently suffered sore eyes, continued to work for the Navy until his patron James II fled the country.

A Problem with Dates

In Stuart Times, England together with other protestant countries still used the *Julian Calendar*, set in motion by Julius Caesar. To allow for the fact that there is not an exact number of days in a year, an extra day was added every four years. However, this did not correct the error sufficiently and by the 1500's, a discrepancy of 10 days grew up. This was causing problems with religious festivals especially Easter and so Pope Gregory proposed that Thursday October 4, 1582 should be followed by Friday October 15. This *Gregorian Calendar* was accepted by catholic countries but not by protestant ones. Dates in France were therefore 10 days in advance of England.

Other countries changed to the Gregorian Calendar later, with England and Scotland both doing so in 1752. Historians and scientists now write all dates in the Gregorian form. For instance, the total eclipse of the sun took place in London on April 8, 1652, but a calendar in Lucy Townsend's room said March 29, 1652. In either case it was still called *Black Monday!*

Monday 29th. March, 1652 = *Monday 8th. April, 1652*

Tuesday 20th. January, 1648 = *Tuesday 30th. January, 1649*

In England, the New Year started on March 25, whereas in Scotland and on the Continent it started on January 1.

The day on which the King was executed was called January 20, 1648 in England, but January 30, 1649 in France. Under the Gregorian Calendar, it was already 1649 but in protestant England it was still 1648. Charles I was King of both England and Scotland and to add to the confusion, he was executed in one country in 1648 and in the other in 1649. However they were both protestant, so both considered it to be January 20. All was harmonised in 1752.

King Charles I

Charles was born in1600 and was a weak and backward child. He only became heir to the Throne when his elder brother Prince Henry died in 1612. At the Coronation in 1625, his diminutive figure, quiet dignity and sad handsome face impressed everyone. A loving, faithful, husband and father, Charles set a high standard of behaviour and manners at Court, not by decree but by example. In matters of government, however, his behaviour was often devious and arrogant as he tried to impose his will and to act upon his belief in *The Divine Right of Kings* to govern as he wished. For ten years he ruled and imposed taxes without Parliament and the inevitable clash led to the civil wars. After seven years of victories and defeats, it ended with his execution at Whitehall in January 1649. Charles was the most enlightened patron of the Arts and his collection of Italian Renaissance paintings forms the basis of the National Gallery in London.

Queen Henrietta Maria

The daughter of the French King, Henry IV, and Catherine de Medici, she did not impress the young prince Charles when he visited the French Court disguised as plain Mr. Smith on his way to collect a bride in Spain. The Spanish trip ended in disaster and a few years later it was Henrietta Maria who became Queen of England. She was courageous and determined in her desire to help her husband but her political intriguing for foreign help were more than a little damaging. When the Parliamentary victories made it obvious that Charles was in danger of losing everything, he sent the Queen and his younger children back to France for safety. After the execution of her husband, she never gave up her struggle to help her son. She lived in poverty and distress in exile until the restoration in 1660. However, the last years of her life were spent in comfortable retirement in England.

King Charles II

A mixture of Scots, Danish, French and Italian blood made Charles II rather odd to look at by the standards of his time. He grew to be exceptionally tall and swarthy, something which must have seemed strange to those who knew his father. Some years after his restoration Charles looked into a mirror. "Odd's fish" he said "I am an ugly fellow." Charles spent his youth in frustrating, poverty-striken exile, always planning to regain the Crown and sometimes attempting it. A final disastrous attempt ended with defeat at the battle of Worcester and his narrow, but sensational, escape from arrest and almost certain death.

In 1660, things took a turn for the better and he was invited to return to become a *Constitutional Monarch* amid great scenes of public rejoicing. Charles's easy going manner and fondness for women set the racy style of Restoration society. It was witty, extravagant, permissive and yet took an intelligent and informed interest in science and the arts.

William and Mary

Mary, the eldest daughter of James II was tall, dark and vivacious, so when, in 1677, she was told by her father and step mother that she was to marry her cousin, Prince William of Orange, she wept for two days. He was hardly an attractive match. William was asthmatic, hunchbacked and much shorter than her. It seemed also that she would have to lead a lonely life in Holland. However, the marriage turned out much better than she expected.

William, when he was not engrossed in politics and military campaigning, was a connoisseur of the arts and Mary found this side of his nature a great joy. Together, with the help of Daniel Marot, they created superb gardens and palatial buildings. When her father fled to France with his wife and newborn son she was invited to become Queen of England. She refused to rule as sole sovereign and so she and William were crowned as joint rulers. Mary died from smallpox in 1694, because a man she had touched while performing the ceremony of *Touching for the King's Evil*, had the disease.

Lucy Townsend is acting as Lady in Waiting to the Countess of Newcastle at Welbeck Abbey while her husband is abroad. When her hosts entertain King Charles I and Queen Henrietta Maria at Bolsover Castle her sons act in the masque devised for the occasion by the playwright Ben Johnson. In 1634 Bolsover Castle is in the process of being built to the design of the architect John Smythson.

Lucy Townsend
30th. July, 1634
Welbeck

Returned to Welbeck flushed with the children's triumph but much worn with preparation for Ralph last night and the early rising.

Their Majesties were received at Bolsover by the Earl and Countess but our advance journey was entirely too early for my chicks, who played little cupids in the Masque and had to be rehearsed and dressed before the Royal guests' arrival.

The morning certainly started ill. Little Ralph tripped over a bucket left carelessly by the builders. He came screaming that he had broke his arm and how could he play before the King now? I near swooned, but when dear Captain Jackson showed him a candy, he moved his arm quick enough!

Ralph received a bite more than the candy from my hand and so there were more tears and tantrums. The rehearsals left much to be desired. Mr. Johnson's piece was flimsy stuff and I thought must have wounded Mr. Smythson, though he managed to laugh with good grace. I can only assume the suddenness of the visit of their majesties had left His Lordship little time in London to advise his chosen poet, who must remain a'bed and so can neither attend his Lordship nor write with the vigour he once did.

The Queen's appearance in matching gown and dress of pearly green seemed so charming and simple, although entirely worked with seed pearls and diamonds. She quite outshone us all I estimate the gown will have taken at least fourteen yards of silk thus wrought. My mind spins at such vast expense! Fashion, on these occasions, demands great sacrifice from its devotees, men as well as women, but such pleasure and employment are gained that we are all happy to submit to her decrees.

So much money has again been spent, I wonder what state my patrons will be in. Two Royal visits within a year! Few could sustain it. The lavishness of the spectacle and the novelty of the building, unfinished though it is, made the King well pleased.

The boys looked so pretty in their perukes and buskins together with their bows and quivers. This transformed, wondrously, two earthbound brats (for that is what most often they are!) into the divinest of baby gods.

Ralph in the presence of the Queen overcame all anxiety and played his part with the greatest sweetness and presented her majesty with her banquet without a tremor of nerves.

The Masque at Bolsover

The Earl of Newcastle   King Charles I   Queen Henrietta Maria   The Countess of Newcastle

CUT ALONG THIS LINE

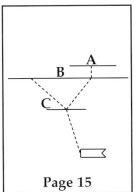

Score along the dotted lines and cut out these pieces while looking at this side of the paper.

Cut along the blue outline. Do not cut any closer to the figures.

Glue the pieces to page 15 in alphabetical order and then link them with thread as shown in the diagram.

PULL TAG

The Masque at Bolsover

The Masque at Bolsover

The Cupids

Captain Jackson & Lucy Townsend

Page 15

This diagram shows how the thread links the three pieces so that they will pull up together and make a three-dimensional scene.

Start with the backmost piece and sew through the pairs of points. Go through them several times so that the thread does not slip. They are marked ○ ○

Allow enough thread between the pieces so that it is taut when the figures lie flat.

Glue the pull tag to a short piece of thread at the front.

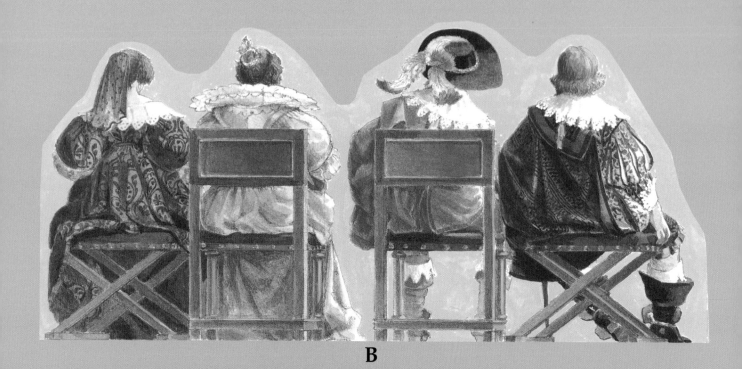

B

D

D

C

A

Poor Henry stumbled slightly at the King's feet and only just managed to suppress his tears, with the help of a kind word from His Majesty. I was behind My Lady and with heart thumping against my tight lacing, near swooned when the boys seemed to forget their speeches.

I have just discovered that my fidgety hands have quite ruined one of my best galants. I must have presented myself to the King and Queen in these tatters! When will I ever grow out of such girlishness?

My only consolation is that My Lord of Newcastle seemed in equal discomfort. At least until Henry remembered his line "Another Cupid?" and their little play began. The Queen was especially charmed by Ralph and gave him a kiss. This made him pink cheeked and speechless at last! A Queen's kiss may prove fortunate, God will it.

I am quite in love with the corner fireplace in the Heaven Closet, so novel and practical in a confined space. I must ask Mr Smythson about one for my own little room.

Tomorrow I am released from my duties here and we all return to Alstonefield. Henry is thrilled that Captain Jackson promises to teach him fly fishing in the next few weeks. No doubt I will have little chance to visit the Dove, Stanshope or Blore. Oh to be a man!

I was told some news of my Husband. It seems he has found service with the King's nephew, Prince Rupert of the Rhine. He therefore seems occupied a little more to my honour than before, though I could have wished him home in England. May God preserve him and bring him back to his proper duties !

The Countess has presented me with a hair ornament of little silver gilt flowers, a gift she says of gratitude for my friendship and service in the past stressful days. It looks very similar to her majesty's and I am sure I will never be able to wear it for fear of losing it.

Ralph Townsend
22nd. & 23rd. October, 1642
Oxfordshire

Ralph - a cupid at Bolsover eight years earlier, is now 16 and a student at Oxford. His father, although in the service of Prince Rupert, is still fighting abroad, so his mother Lucy has taken charge of family affairs. She now lives with her children in the countryside not far from Oxford. Here, Ralph writes this diary entry after what will probably be the most eventful day of his life. The civil war in England has just broken out and the royalist forces under King Charles and his nephew Prince Rupert are lining up against the Parliamentary forces close to the village of Radway. What became known as the battle of Edgehill is about to begin.

Up betimes yesterday and studied. While trying to think what to wear I darned my stockings. The townsmen were busy fortifying the town against the King! Tom burst in as I completed my dressing, "Never mind your cadenettes or your galants - lay off your gown! Tis war! Furnish yourself for the King or be held a coward!" So saying, or rather screaming, he thrust my pot on my head and ran off to rouse others for the King.

I grabbed my sword and my father's cuirass in haste and ran out into the quadrangle and through into the town. Dorcus was not pleased to be taken from his feeding and Mun did everything to delay me, saying the saddle was not clean etc. I rode off in high excitement without it. Many left their gowns at the Town Gate in the gaiety of leaving their lessons.

It was only as we approached Radway and first heard the noise of battle, that I knew I was afraid and drew rein. I was determined to stay an observer but Tom laughed at my fear and, shouting, rode on with the others to join the fray. Dorcus plunged forward to keep up with them and I was unable to stop him as we rushed into the battle. Nothing I could do changed his course until, his belly ripped open by the pike of a wounded trooper, he let out a fearful scream and fell dead under me. I struggled to free myself and, as I got up, someone threw himself at me. I had no understanding of his purpose and plunged my sword into his side, I know not how. He called out "Ralph!" and fell. I then saw it was our neighbour, Mr Bishop, my father's friend. Unable to dissengage my sword and near senseless, I saw the King, at a distance. Yet he appeared strangely vivid in the confusion of my mind, dressed in a black velvet coat lined with ermine. His face seemed drawn with sadness urging me to go to him but I could not move ...

... A voice behind claimed me his prisoner and I was led off, still stupefied, by a young soldier. As we reached the safety of a hedge, I recovered a little. My captor looked closely at me and although dressed as a man, it was Mistress Ellen Blackstay! At the instant we recognised each other, Ellen was shot through the head and slumped forward on to my lap. I remember nothing more ...

... It was dark and bitter cold when I recovered to find myself being stripped of my clothes, as if one of the surrounding dead. I leapt up and ran and ran. At last I found myself at home. I know not how unless it be by God's providence. Mother wept and scolded all at the same time but I pushed past and have now locked myself in my room.

Never, never, never again will I seek adventure! Oh God, let me remain a snivelling coward and take away the stench of death! I cannot stop weeping. Little Anne is fatherless and to think we all thought it an adventure!

Here at Edgehill, the King and a cavalry officer survey the fighting. Even when actually on the battlefield, the two are very splendidly attired. The officer is wearing a cuirass and a helmet and the King may well have some armour under his fashionable coat. The King probably also has a steel lining to the crown of his hat. Although these items offered little real protection against the effects of firearms, they might save a life or injury in some circumstances. Armour was very expensive to buy and so it was mostly worn as a badge of rank.

Ralph Townsend's letter to his mother Lucy
18th. February, 1652

Madam,

We have just arrived in Antwerp from the turmoils in Paris. I write in haste and not without vexation.

You will now see how foolish your admonitions would have proved, had I heeded them. It is thanks to my lavish style, not to your penny pinching, that I can now inform you of my marriage to Hortense Fleurville, the prettiest woman in Paris and heiress to the Fleurville estates. At a blow I please the mercenary side, as well as the natural part of my nature!

Tomorrow, at your insistence, I will see the Earl of Newcastle. You see, Madam, that not all your lectures go unheeded! The Earl and Countess live here in great magnificence, entirely on credit, housed in a palace that once belonged to that much respected artist, Sir Peter Paul Rubens.

I have had three new suits made in Paris, each with a matching casaque in the latest style and have no doubt that these credentials will impress the Earl. I have your letter of introduction, should I require it and expect to gain favour and employment suitable for my station.

I shall make my first visit tomorrow wearing my dead monkey coloured silk trimmed with blue ribbons and silver lace. Then on the next visit, my black and gold trimmed with scarlet. For my establishment I will wear the silver lace and pearl suit, lined in silk the colour of the cheeks of Venus.

My wife sends her greetings and begs you to consider her as your true loving daughter.

Beware the darkening of the sun expected in London. Our appeal against sequestration coincides with the omens and I doubt that Colonel Philip is as influential as he pretends.

I trust you have not mentioned my recent visit and the blackboy's escape. You must send all the money you can lay your hands on. Every day I am pestered for payments.

My wife's family cannot provide her dowry till their case be taken up. Mark me well, only my appearance will hold our family from eclipse and ensure credit. No more of your parsimony, I beg!

I remain, Madam
Your true admiring son

Ralph Townsend

PS. This messenger needs no reward, so do not waste money on needless generosity.

Black Monday at the Court of Appeal

Score along the dotted lines and cut out these pieces while looking at this side of the paper.

Cut along the purple ouline. Do not cut any closer to the figures.

Glue the pieces to page 21 in alphabetical order and then link them with thread as shown in the diagram.

A Swooning Lady

Lucy Townsend & A Lady Petitioner

Black Monday at the Court of Appeal

Black Monday at the Court of Appeal

PULL TAG

Page 21

A
  B
  C
D

This diagram shows how the thread links the four pieces so that they will pull up together and make a three-dimensional scene.

Start with the backmost piece and sew through the pairs of points. Go through them several times so that the thread does not slip. They are marked ○ ○

Allow enough thread between the pieces so that it is taut when the figures lie flat.

Glue the pull tag to a short piece of thread at the front.

The Lady Armide Streager & Her Page

A Young Man

CUT ALONG THIS LINE

B

A

E E

D

C

Lucy Townsend
29th. March, 1652 (Black Monday)
London

I had but little sleep during the night. Thoughts and plans of how to present my case and my son's unkind letter prevented my rest.

I must have slept somewhat because the mournful barks of the dogs interrupted a strange dream and they continued until I could bear it no more. What were the servants doing, still asleep at seven? I rose and wrapped myself in a blanket to keep warm but needed a second before I dared venture out to rouse the house. All, it seems were in a great fear of our fortunes, because of the eclipse promised for ten this morning.

I must own that all their superstitions and the alarums of the dogs put my own faith out of confidence and my temper was consequently quite put out. My appearance was not till ten-thirty but I designed to be dressed and calm to review my case, well before it was time to leave our lodgings. My dress, long since planned, was hurried in by Sarah and immediately my mind was filled with doubts. Was this severity too much against my character? Would I not be more effective in the softer authority of a gentlewoman?

Sarah was of little help, remarking that Mistress Overlay had lost all by her extravagance and that My Lady Olstead gained nothing by her Pribiterian dress.

Mun came with the letter I had prayed for. My dear Guardian assured me that he had made strong and, he thought, successful representations to the judges, provided that I presented a dutiful and sober appearance to the court. From anyone else I would have gone against it, but from such a loyal friend and one so influential, I fell into an unaccustomed meekness and wore the dress that had been prepared.

I made entry to the court waiting room a full hour before I was to be heard. Several other cases were to be presented, almost all by members of our weaker sex. A nervous whispering discovered each identity. Many were high born with husbands and sons exiled as delinquents.

The Lady Armide Streager went in before me, her husband having strangely vanished after Worcester and all his lands taken by Parliament. She was dressed grandly in black silk taffety, her tailor has great skill in the cutting of gowns. Her dramatic appearance was much enhanced by a scarlet scarf that fell from beneath her lace kerchief band and a tall hat trimmed with cock feathers. No one has ever looked more daunting.

However, just as I was told to prepare myself to go in, her case was coming to verdict and I heard her voice scream out "Oh villains you are damned!" She repeated this seven times and each time it became darker. She rushed out past us all and the court was thrown into confusion. Many next to me screaming that we had all been bewitched. Others swooned, thinking that the end of the world was upon us. It was, I own, highly disturbing, though the eclipse had been foretold.

When light and calm had been restored, I was able to make my pleas and the judges were well disposed towards me. Whether it was the majesty of nature or the intervention of Colonel Philip that had impressed the minds of those present, or perhaps just my unaccustomed mildness and simple elegance of dress, I shall never know. Whatever the cause, I returned to my lodging in possession of all but our London property. Which being in a state of ruin, I warrant is well worth the losing.

I shall order a hat like Lady Streager! It will suit my defiant nature. I am told she has been taken as a witch! Poor woman, may God preserve her.

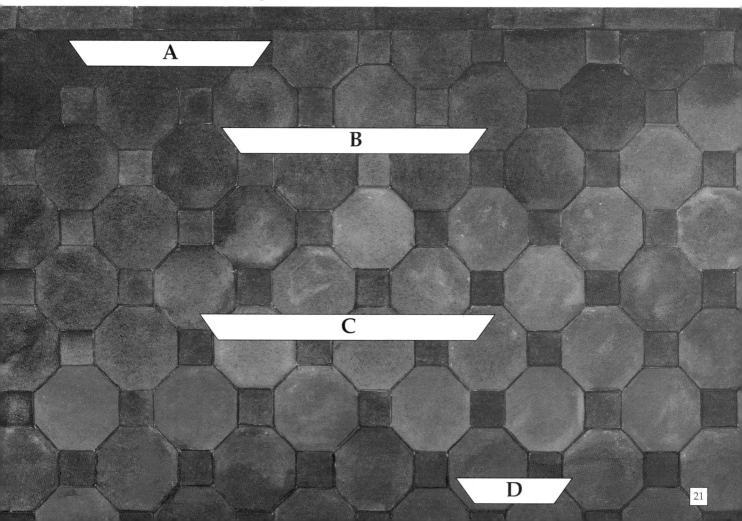

Ralph Townsend
17th. October, 1666
London

Up early, roused by the fall of timber. Meerman's house is being
cleared at last. Soot and dust everywhere but how light the room is
now. I remained in my night-gown to see the view of devastation as
the dust subsided.

James had put out my best lawn shirt with Venetian lace on sleeve
and front, an excellent choice. However, when I decided to dress,
everything he had placed at my disposal, including my drawers, were
completely covered in soot and dust. All had to be replaced. I had
just dropped a clean shirt over my head and was in the act of
arranging the sleeves when Anne burst in with my clean drawers. A
pretty young woman but she must learn some modesty. James,
resentful of my complaint for leaving my best shirt uncovered, was
ungenerous with the perfume and careless with the razor as he
shaved me.

Decided on the apricot stockings, only to find the heel of one was
holed but none of the others could be considered with the suit I was
determined to wear - silver grey, broidered with roses - so put them
on anyway.

The clock struck twelve, throwing me into a panic and I thrust my
self into the breeches and petticoats that Anne held out for me - only
to find that I had put both legs in the left leg of my rhinegreaves - this
is not the first time this has happened. Mercifully, I discovered the
mistake before I left my room and so saved myself from the embar-
rassment of a second twitting from Mr. Pepys.

*"This day the King begins to put on his vest,
and I did see several persons of the House of Lords,
and Commons too, great courtiers, who are in it."*
Samuel Pepys, 15th. October, 1666

As I left the house I saw Meerman in what I took to be an over elaborate dust coat and determined to complain of the soot and dust his house had caused. Lest he thought I was debasing myself as I addressed him, I was forced to cover and my peruke was bruised. For the damage to be repaired, James had to wait a full hour. Ld. be praised, that the quarterage is no more than four shillings.

My French doublet and cloak were quite the best I had seen but stap me, on entering Whitehall, everyone of quality was dressed like Meerman! Lucy tells me they are called Persian Vests and Mr. Evelyn is responsible for introducing them to His Majesty. Apparently the King says he will admit no other.

I must order one immediately. James does not deserve to be given the doublet but I doubt that the cape will be sufficient to make up in the Persian style.

Hortense was told by Lord Newcombe Facet that this so called Persian style is as French as the fashions they have outmoded. The French King, it seems, has invented a coat which only his privileged friends can wear. Only those given a written paper from the King can wear this blue and silver coat called the *juste-au-corps à brevet*. I must order one immediately. Stap me - I must.

A letter from Jackson has quite spoilt my humour. Having been so great and prodigal he now implores the return of his loan. One thing I thought the conflagration had done was to release me from worries about debts. Everywhere I am told that papers and contracts have burned but this bumpkin with his papers intact remains to harass me. I shall have to pay him, or endure my mother's lecturers which I cannot.

Hortense Townsend
17th. October, 1666
London

I was awoken by Anne, looking very flushed. She told me that Mr. Townsend was up and dressing and we were to leave by noon.

She said that Mr Meerman's house is all down and the front rooms covered in soot. It took over an hour to leave instruction for the cleaning.

At eleven I was helped into my chemise. Its perfume is charming and cheered me greatly. As I stepped into my under petticoat, I stumbled slightly and managed to tear some of the pleating at the waist. Anne had to run and fetch the red silk. In fact it looked even more charming than the first and better compliments my stockings.

My bodice took much effort to lace to my satisfaction but, at last, my flesh submitted to the joint wills of Anne and myself. I nearly fainted with the exertion and had to recover myself before the paint was applied to my face and breast.

Anne has arranged my hair so charmingly today, that I resolved not to have it cut and made into a wig, even though they are so fashionable and pretty. My hair being done, I stepped into my over petticoat, skirted with black bobbin lace. The effort last night of sewing it on is well rewarded.

Anne bent her nail back trying to pass the waistband under the busk and I had to complete the task myself. I offered to let her use my smelling salts and as I got these from the dressing table, I caught sight of my face in the mirror! The arrangement of patches struck me as highly questionable for St James's.

I was just about to re-arrange them when Mr. Townsend burst into the room, saying he must patch his face or be taken for a bumpkin. James had dropped his patches into the shaving water and he must use mine!

Whitehall and St James's was charming. All the Quality were there and I felt quite one of them in my new gown.

Mr. Townsend, poor sweet, seemed much put out at being outmoded in a doublet and cloak but I persuaded him to let me stay an hour or two longer to represent him with the Quality. Lord Newcome Facet was very attentive. Oh quels moments jolis à Paris!

Anne is becoming markedly interested in my husband and I must insist on her departure. I will be a laughing stock else! Mr. Townsend has been very kind to her and her family since that dreadful day. But enough is enough! Others too lost their fathers in the war. I am sans smelling salts and why is that? Because of my uncontrollable generosity of spirit. Who else would allow that girl the use of such an essential commodity?!

Henpen has just shown me a drawing he has done - Lord what a precocious talent! When I pressed for an explanation he replied "Tis Lot with his daughters, madam as you must know. Mr. Drawell has taught me how to depict flesh, both young and old." I must speak with firmness to that young man! Lot's daughters indeed, and the boy is only eight. 'Tis a passing good drawing, I must own. Mr. Townsend must not see it.

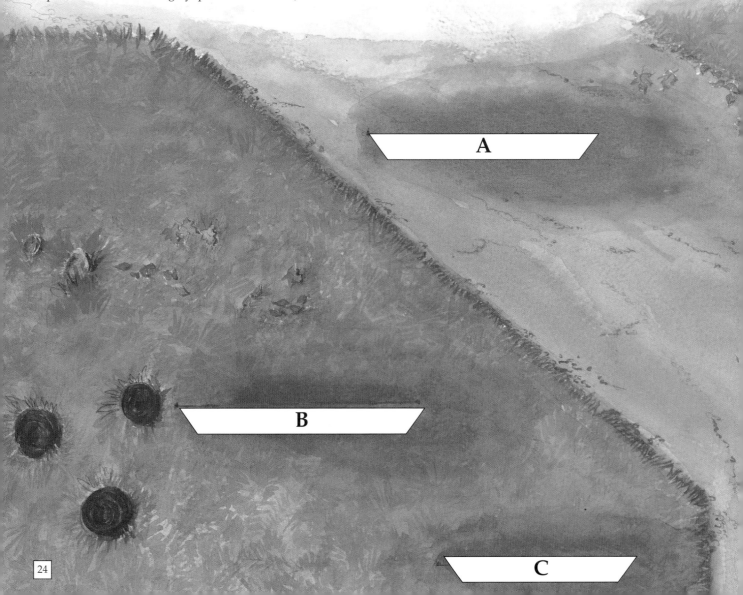

A

B

C

A Young Man & his Dog

Duke & Duchess of Willicombe

PULL TAGS

Whitehall & St James's

Whitehall & St James's

Whitehall & St James's

Whitehall & St James's

✂

Score along the dotted lines and cut out these pieces while looking at this side of the paper.

Cut along the green ouline. Do not cut any closer to the figures.

Glue the pieces to pages 24 & 27 in alphabetical order and then link them with thread as shown in the diagram on page 29.

A Young Couple

Newcombe Facet

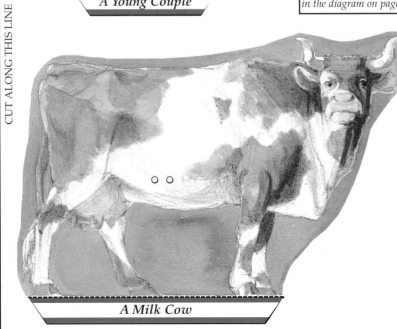

A Milk Cow

Hortense Townsend

A

C

G G H H

D

F

E

B

St James's Park

D

E

F

Henpen, Ralph and Hortense's son Henry, is now grown up and, following his early promise, is working as an artist. He feels he never quite receives the recognition he deserves. Two artists are much favoured by William and Mary: Marot the Frenchman best remembered for his designs for the gardens at Hampton Court and Verrio the Italian who specialised in allegorical paintings on walls and ceilings.

The reign of William and Mary is drawing to a close. Mary has carried out an ancient royal tradition known as Touching for the King's Evil. It was thought that if someone with the disease scrofula could touch the monarch, he or she would be cured. Unfortunately the man hoping for a cure and who was touched by the Queen had smallpox.

Henry Townsend
27th. December, 1694
London

Could not sleep during the night for thoughts of depicting Alexander and Xerxes, so was up by five and made composition studies until ten. None satisfactory.

I left Josiah and Will to arrange the studio for today's sitting with Madame la Comtesse and, being ill-humoured, decided to walk to see what progress was made in the City. There are still construction sheds round St Paul's. All talk was of the poor Queen's illness . Touching for *The King's Evil* has put her in mortal danger herself. Many people are apprehensive for their future but others have secret hopes of advancement.

In Ruffs coffee house I drank a deal of coffee and spoke unwisely and loudly of my own ambitions. Why am I always impolitic after frustrations with my muse?

Returned home in time to prepare myself for yet another distracting sitting with Madame la Comtesse de Manqué. She arrived two hours late. I could hardly contain my displeasure and to cap it all she had chosen to wear a mantua and fontanges entirely at odds with the concept we had agreed.

She sent her man off to collect the proper dress. I'm sure this was her intent and she chatted away gaily, giving her charming French opinions about the Queen's love of porcelain and tulips, comparing the royal collections in France and England.

My ill-humour began to vanish when she expressed her mighty admiration for the uncommon magnificence of my furniture, saying she must have it for herself. We conversed in this charming manner, she with her smiles and French ways and I more inclined to bask in her perfections, until after half an hour her man returned with the most excellent wine and the dress we had settled on for her appearance as Venus.

Whilst she changed into the goddess, the Comtesse related an amusing tale about the investiture of the Order of St Esprit some years ago, before she arrived in this country. Apparently one distinguished recipient was unable to pull the side of his wig into its proper position. For some reason it had twisted round to the back and his cheek was left exposed for the entire ceremony. Better still, three Knights had stood too close together and had become inextricably entangled together through the snagging of various hooks, swords and the excessive amount of lace distributed on their costume! They had to be torn apart before the ceremony could continue , to the amusement of all. These events conspired to turn the gravest of French occasions into a comedy worthy of Voltaire himself.

The painting of *Venus* has not turned out well so far but the Comtesse is returning tomorrow morning so that I may further render her flesh with the glow necessary to achieve a successful representation.

A Sitting at Henpen's Studio

✂

Score along the dotted lines and cut out these pieces while looking at this side of the paper.

Cut along the pink ouline. Do not cut any closer to the figures.

Glue the pieces to page 31 in alphabetical order and then link them with thread as shown in the diagram.

Josiah the Monkey

Madame La Comtesse de Manqué

CUT ALONG THIS LINE

A Sitting at Henpen's Studio   A Sitting at Henpen's Studio

PULL TAG

Henry (Henpen) Townsend

Page 24	Page 27

These diagrams show how the thread links the pieces on pages 24, 27 & 31 so that they will pull up together and make a three-dimensional scene.

Start with the backmost piece and sew through the pairs of points. Go through them several times so that the thread does not slip. They are marked ○ ○

Allow enough thread between the pieces so that it is taut when the figures lie flat.

Glue the pull tag to a short piece of thread at the front.

Page 31

B

A

D   D

C

Henry (Henpen) Townsend
28th, December, 1694
London

I have just been told of the Queen's death at one o'the clock this morning. The Court is in total disarray and my charming Comtesse will not come today.

I have ordered a set of mourning clothes, fur lined and a great coat against the extreme cold. Cutwell promises all will be ready the day after tomorrow, but not sooner, as black cloth is now in great demand.

Unable to be abroad without mourning. I have instructed the servants to say I have an acute ague after walking out yesterday in the cold wind.

Indeed, 'tis somewhat true. Thought of the Comtesse made me careless of the winter and I have become uncommon stiff. My shoes are stained beyond revival and Beaulast took them saying that he despairs of repairing the heel I dislodged.

I must stop, all news is of gloom and frigidity, the ink freezes in the pot and my fingers ache. My drawing is reduced to the mediocrity of Verrio - perhaps worse!

1634

1645

1645

1666

1690

1690